A Praise the Lord series book

Finding Faith

Wellness through stories of hope and love

By Michelle Lovato

Michelle Lovato

Copyright 2018 by Michelle Lovato
and Boutique Books. P.O. BOX 1664, Bigfork MT 59911

All rights reserved. No part of this book may be reproduced in any form or by any electronic or mechanical means, including information storage of retrieval systems without express written permission from the publisher.

Boutique Books

A Praise the Lord series book

Finding Faith

Wellness through stories of hope and love

By Michelle Lovato

Finding Faith: Wellness through stories of hope and love is dedicated to my mom, Patricia Brander.
You are my inspiration, encouragement and mentor. I love you

Michelle Denise Brander Lovato

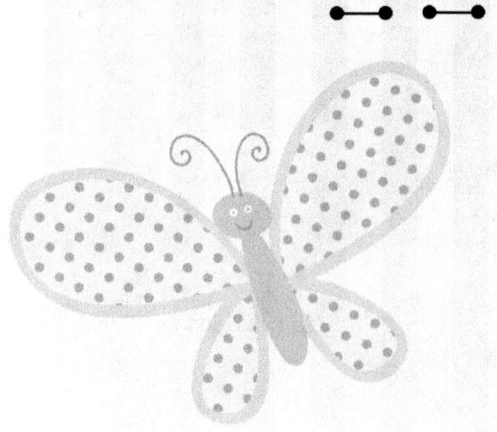

Dear Reader,

This gift book and journal is created as a blessing. God loves you and wants to interact with you. Finding Faith: Wellness through stories of hope and love is intended to spark your memories and remind you how God moved in your life through during your lifetime.

Finding Faith: Wellness through stories of hope and love is the first in my new Interactive Community Publishing Initiative, which is explained in full at the back of this book.

I encourage you to read it, enjoy it, and buy copies for your friends, girl groups and churches.

Feel free to contact me anytime at submissions.findingfaith@gmail.com.

Michelle Lovato

My Sucess Does Not Come Without God & Friends

I want to start this book with a special thank you to the smart, loving men and women of Inspired Working Women of Kalipsell at Canvas Church, Calvery Chapel of Flathead Valley, Mountain Song Church of Bigfork, Calivery Chapel Green Valley of Henderson, NV, Apple Valley Baptist Church in California, First Baptist Church of Watsonville, CA and MacGregor and Luedeke Literary Agency of Manzanita, Oregon.

A special thanks to Chip MacGregor, Vince Lovato, Pearl Galbraith, Joi Gratney, Linnea Gerspach,, Joe Monto, Heidi Barnes, and Patricia Brander.

Table of Contents

God Has The Cure For Cancer	13
Bad Singing, Good Heart	19
Of Diapers And Daddies	25
Summer Days Make Me Feel ... Like Passing Out	31
Spring Doe	37
Ride Baby Ride	45
Dad Had A Choice	51
Jesus Is A Super Friend	59

Table of Contents

Closer Than A Brother	67
Rest For The Weary	75
Stinky Slinky	81
Funky Fellowship Is A Family Friend	87
Free To Run To Jesus	93
Not So Big After all	99
Jail house Rock	105
Twists Of Faith	111
Personal Space	117
Cheap Chocolate No Match For Jesus	123
My Perfect Mother's Day	129
Of Mops And Mommies	137

Joyful In Hope	143
Art For The Aged	149
Comfort Zone	157
The Case Of The Bully Chihuahuas	163
Safety Is At The Crossroads	169
Want to be in the next Finding Faith?	175
Writer's Guidelines	177
What Are You Looking For?	179
Practice Makes .. Better	183
My Way, His Way	187

God Has The Cure For Cancer

1 Peter 1:22 (NIV)
Now that you have purified yourselves by obeying the truth so that you have sincere love for your brothers, love one another deeply, from the heart.

By Michelle Lovato

It was a dim December morning the day I dropped onto the living room couch next to my three young girls and told them their grandmother had malignant cancer.

The muted sun managed to penetrate the clouds and infiltrate a window next to me despite my longing to prevent it.

Surgery was an urgent priority. And then there was the matter of finding someone to give blood.

It wasn't me.

Oh, how I wish that it

could have been me. Helplessly I sat there with the girls, bent over myself wondering what I could do to help the one woman in the world I could not bear to lose.

Sadness swam in the sunbeams around me as the girls witnessed their mother grasping for words to comfort them.

Shortly after I stopped talking, my eldest daughter spoke up. "She can have my blood," she said.

A few days later my youngest handed me two of her most prized stuffed animals.

"They are so Grandma has something to hold in the hospital."

My baby girl would not sleep without

them, but Grandma needed them more.

Right behind her stood my middle daughter. A customary good-bye embrace was in order as I was preparing to accompany my mother to the doctor.

When we touched, my sweet little lamb grabbed me by the waist and held me so tight I thought she might just burn her tiny little soul into my weakened legs.

"Give my love to Grandma," she said.

As adults we often become jaded.

When something bad happens we just want to slouch over and cry, to give up and give in to the seemingly overwhelming sense of grief we are experiencing. But God uses these episodes, like the scare of

Cancer in our lives, to show us Himself and all His incredible ability; to prove that He has the power to supply our needs and to soothe our aching souls. And isn't it funny, that often, God uses the purity of a child to showcase some of His greatest handiwork.

Father, Healer,
Thank You for looking past the medical ailments in my life and rooting out the cancer in my insincere devotion to You. You are so Holy.
Thank you, Lord. I love you.

Now it is your turn. Share a scare in your life and the marvelous grace God showed you in your time of need.

Michelle Lovato

Whether you are riddled with cancer or saturated with good health, give your thanks to God.

Father Healer,

Bad Singing, Good Heart

Ephesians 2: 8-9 (NIV)
For it is by grace you have been saved, through faith; and this is not from yourselves; it is the gift of God, not by works, so that no one can boast.

By Michelle Lovato

Anyone in my family will be happy to confirm that I have many wonderful talents, none of which are in the area of music. Let's just say my body moves to the beat of a different drummer, and my voice sounds much better when nothing comes out.

Thankfully, I attend a loving, accepting church, whose motto is:

"If you don't sing well,
Sing that much louder."

Every Sunday morning, the faithful crew that comprises our congregation gathers to shout to the Lord in a variety of different keys and tones.

    And I have to admit, even though I am usually happily howling out to the Lord, it is by the grace of God we form a melody that is a sweet serenade to our Heavenly Father.

    Praise God that He doesn't expect us to seek his approval through the works of our hands or the polished echoes that flow forth from our mouths.

    For it is by grace that we have been saved. And it is when we learn to accept that the sacrifices of Jesus' death on the cross is God's free gift to mankind, and that it was provided as a bridge built by the Master Shepherd for the sheep of his fold, that we can

begin to comprehend the power of God's grace.

It is not because of our works that God allowed for the death of Jesus. It is because of the unconditional love God possesses for mankind, his longing to connect, his desire to remove the barrier of sin that stood between us and our father, that he provided his sacrificial gift of Jesus.

Though I may spend my life attempting to improve on the sounds that travel up my throat and through my lips, it is comforting to know that it won't determine my eternity.

It is my request that Jesus Christ live in my heart and move in my life, that set God in motion to bless me with His grace.

Lord of Grace,
Thank You that Your mercy and love are everlasting. You are the author of love and have provided the perfect atonement to bridge the gap between our sin and Your presence. Thank you for your free gift.
I love you.

Now it is your turn. What was it about the day you turned your life over to God that spurred you to action? Do you remember the void you felt before that decision and the rich satisfaction and calm you felt afterward? Share your experience.

Thank God for all He has done in your life. Thank Him for reminding you that you are not left o sludge through life alone.

Lord of Grace.

Of Diapers and Daddies

1 Thes 5: 16-18 (NASB)
Be joyful always; pray without ceasing. Give thanks in all circumstances, for this is God's will for you in Christ Jesus.

By Michelle Lovato

Ever seen what three little kids can do to a father playfully taunting them on the floor?

They are warriors! Play warriors! And they are on a mission to fight the playful hand opposing them.

Diapered bottoms rise like flags over the soft surface of Daddy's belly.

Shrieking shouts of joy pierce the air like deadly weapons shot at all enemies of fun.

Thankful Mommy is in another room busily

preparing for impending fatigue, bath and bedtime.

Nothing more beautiful could take place within the walls of a family's home.

Giving birth to a child is one of life's most awe-striking events.

And it's always been the goal of my husband and I to provide the best possible childhood for our offspring.

Over the years I've learned that even though some lessons are hard and painful to learn, a sweet smile and warm hug from Mom or Dad seems to take all the pain away and restore that ever-so-precious unquenchable joy that accompanies a happy childhood.

We too are much beloved children of our Heavenly Father, who calls us to look at ourselves as prayer warriors on a mission to fight the evil opposing us.

Though our battles are far more intense than a gentle roll around the living room floor, God gives us the ultimate weapon of prayer to pierce the enemy's heart and silence his attempts to wage spiritual war.

Joyously, we are already victorious through our risen King, Jesus Christ, who gives us the power and the pleasure to be thankful in all circumstances.

And that, after all, is the creator's will for his children in Christ Jesus.

Dear Warrior Lord,

Thank You for being our Warrior King. You are our protector and we call Your name in fun and in danger. Thank you for giving us the medium of prayer to commune in Your Holy presence.

I love you.

Now it is your turn. Share your memories of childhood or childbirth.

Every breath from your heart is thanks to your Warrior Lord. Share the thoughts on your heart with God.

Dear Warrior Lord,

Summer Days Make Me Feel... Like Passing Out

> Jeremiah 31:25 (NIV)
> I will refresh the weary and satisfy the faint.

By Michelle Lovato

Sweltering through another hot Mojave Desert summer, I drove my melting children down Bear Valley Road hoping that I could make it to my husband's office without loosing consciousness.

Already feeling the first dizzying stages of heat stroke; headache, faintness and a mouth folded up like an origami fish - my wet body glistened majestically as the sweat jerky-ed my skin, leaving the faint smell of salt to scent the car.

A funny thought crossed my mind and I smiled as I thanked God that life isn't really like that part in the "Wizard of Oz" story when the wicked witch is doused with water and erupts into steam squealing: "I'm melting, I'm melting."

Choking back a giggle, I reached into the middle of the two front seats and placed my hand on a rapidly disintegrating bag of ice we just purchased.

Immediately, the cool cubes went to work lowering my body temperature, restoring sanity and all brain matter previously altered by the heat.

The ice was an

immediate refreshment for a sad, wilting body in need of replenishment.

Jesus is like that.

He is a cool cube, a refreshing well and a million-dollar air conditioner all wrapped into one wonderful Savior.

I love that when we ask Jesus to guide our lives, affect our daily situations and heal our hurting hearts, he is there, providing on-the-spot and eternal spiritual aid.

Though we may be traveling through a spiritual desert, melting under the heat of a bad situation or jerky-ed because of things in our lives gone wrong, Jesus is an immediate refreshment for a sad, wilting soul.

Father Refresher,

Thank You for knowing my name, for knocking on the door to my heart and for making Your home in me. Thank You for cool summer breezes and simple picture stories that remind me of Your great worth.

Thank you for my life, Lord. I love You.

Now it is your turn. How has God cooled your overheating soul?

Share our refreshing thoughts of praise with our Eternal Spring.

Father Refresher,

Spring Doe

Hebrews 4:16 (NIV)
Let us then approach God's throne of grace with confidence, so that we may receive mercy and find grace to help us in our time of need.

By Michelle Lovato

I felt special; like I was getting away with a particularly mischievous prank as I sat in the backseat of my Aunt Cathy's truck licking an ice cream cone.

At home it was a bitter cold Montana day, and while my rapidly-aging husband stayed in Montana babysitting our brand-new escape-artist puppy, I was in Lake Havasu, Arizona taking off my shoes to play in pooling water, riding around in the backseat with my mom and my aunt in the front seat, and feeling that long-forgotten closeness to nuclear family that disappeared decades ago.

It was different on the home front.

In between several high-speed foot chases for our puppy, my husband laboriously designed our newest community print newspaper.

He toiled with digital-file control, rusty design skills and the delivery system I set up before I left.

I promised him I would carry the dreaded family cell phone I despised while I was away, and more importantly, answer the phone when he called.

But truthfully, my husband is an expert at

being a downer and I was in an upper mood.

I ignored call after call.

Eventually, however, I needed my loving hunny, to put money in my travel account, so I answered his call and put him on speaker which forced him to be nice.

"Spring Doe?" he said sarcastically, fully knowing my maneuver, and his fate.

In unison, my aunt and my mother burst into laughter.

"OH BROTHER!" They squealed.

I laughed along.

"Where might the logo be found?" he asked.

I gave the answer my best shot.

Frankly, I was frustrated that after 25 years of marriage

and working side by side, that we still struggle to communicate such minor things as the location of digital art; especially when I told him twice before I left that I wrote specific instructions to find various graphic treasures and pinned them on the refrigerator..

But, I took a big breath, harnessed my patience, called him my "Big Summer Buck" and repeated its location once more.

For the rest of that wonderful trip to Arizona, my aunt and mother made playful fun of the Spring Doe.

When I returned home my husband revealed the truth.

"Spring Doe," he said, was the opposite of what he really wanted to say.

I wonder if that is how God feels about the way we communicate with Him?

We break our promises, ignore his call, manipulate the circumstances to suit our present desire and only pick up in desperation.

And yet God, in His infinite grace, God always listens.

Elohim My Creator,

Thank you for your overwhelming love that allows me to approach you even after I've played mischievous games.

Thank for you overlooking my antics and my irresponsible

motives, then listening to me, when in desperation I call.

Lord, isn't that what Your great mercy is? Forgive me for abusing Your love for me.

Thank you Lord for my life. I love you.

Now it is your turn. What can you see in your life that illustrates God's love despite your actions?

Share your heart with God your Creator.

Elohim My Creator.

Ride baby, Ride

Haggai 1:5 (NIV)
Now this is what the LORD Almighty says:
"Give careful thought to your ways."

By Michelle Lovato

Some years ago, I walked into the dining room and found my three darling daughters preparing for Vacation Bible School.

The eldest was busy ironing a camping adventure t-shirt transfer onto one of my shirts so she could "borrow" it for the night.

My middle daughter was keeping her company by spinning around on the floor, her foot perched atop a plastic dinner plate.

And my youngest was

dressed in a bathrobe and her sister's high heel shoes, laying on her back and inserting her feet into an empty trash bag she was suppose to be using to collect household trash.

They were having an adventure all right.

Wondering why I may have expected anything different than utter chaos I asked the worst question I could possibly spit out of my mouth:

Just what are you doing?

Instantaneously, each one of my little angels jumped into action, imitating what looked like perfect children.

The eldest reminded

me that she had "borrowed" a shirt with a stain.

Suddenly, she was doing me a favor.

The middle child flashed her famous "I'm-too-cute-to punish" smile and began clearing dishes from the table.

The one under her foot just happened to fall from on high and made an escape, and she felt compelled to stop it.

And the youngest rolled to the trash can and started transferring garbage from the floor to the bag. Inserting her feet in the bag, she said, was simply the best way to ensure the most efficient placement of trash.

Before I became the mother
of moving, breathing, talking,
screaming miniature versions

of myself I was convinced nothing would dumbfounded me.

Of course, that was before.

My mother always told me parenting was like an amusement park ride. The kids try to amuse me and then take me for a ride.

Master of My Universe,

You keep my world spinning and my heart from getting overwhelmed with frustration. Thank you for the smile I hid when dealing with the girls. I love that you gave them such creative personalities.

Thank you for the gift of them. I love you.

Now it is your turn. Do you have creative children, relatives? How do they illuminate your world?

Michelle Lovato

Share a moment with God and remind him how much you love his presence in your life.

Master of My Universe.

Dad had a choice

Luke 2:29-31 (NIV)
Sovereign Lord, as you have promised,
you may now dismiss your servant in peace.
For my eyes have seen your salvation, which
you have prepared in the sight of all nations:

By Michelle Lovato

I was driving down a side road near home one day shortly after my father-in-law died, thinking that it was a good thing I was not subjecting other drivers to my poor automotive skill set on a main street.

Distracted. Confused. Deeply upset.
I passed by the local grocery store and glanced up into the sky.

"God, I tried. I tried so hard," I whispered.

Though my dear father-in-law was a man overflowing with love for his kids. I never saw in the entire time I'd known him any indication that he had a personal relationship with Christ.

In the days preceding his passing, myself and several of his other children came to visit him in the hospital.

I was camped out at the head of his bed stroking his balding scalp slowly, methodically in an attempt to comfort him.

One by one, his children told him the story of God's love, Jesus' sacrifice and eternal promise.

Each one of them asked him if he wanted to accept Jesus Christ as his savior, the same question I asked him

days before.

No one got an answer.

Finally, when his days were done and his mission on Earth complete, God called my father-in-law home. And as he passed into eternity I was left with deep despair that this man I loved so dearly might not ascend to the eternal heaven.

As I slowed my car and approached a stop sign, a breath-taking vice grip heaved and pressed against my chest so heavily I cried out.

"I tried God. I tried so hard."

    It's none of my business to
    know the secret thoughts
      between God and man, but

I could not help but wonder if he would ever meet Jesus.

It occurred to me in that moment of sorrow how dearly I wished that I knew if he chose to know Christ.

"I am so glad I am not you God," I whispered. I am devastated that no matter how hard we tried to share your love with this man, it appears to me that he turned his back on you"

I took a breath and waited.

"If this is what it feels like as one small human being in grief, what enormous sorrow must you carry every time you call out to me and get no

answer:"

 The God of all eternity, calling my name just like he called my father-in-law's name before me. The God of the beginning and end calling all our names, over and over until the ultimate moment of death and possible eternal separation.

 God loves us humans so much that he took a scenario of permanent separation between himself and us, and created a connection.

 God sent his one and only son to die on a cross to pay for all of our sins.

 God built that bridge. God made that call.

 But there is a catch.

 God gave each one of us a choice to answer his call.

Dear Alpha and Omega,

Thank you. Thank you. Thank you. Thank you for calling and calling and calling. Forgive me for ignoring and I implore you, please call me some more.

Thank you, Lord. I love you.

Now it is your turn. Has God been calling you? Are you ignoring Him?

Share you grief, your joy and your heart with God.

Dear Alpha and Omega,

Jesus Is A Super Friend

Ephesians 2:10 (NIV)
For we are God's handiwork created in Christ Jesus to do good works, which God prepared in advance for us to do.

By Michelle Lovato

I don't know many little girls who don't secretly long to be a cartoon superhero.

But unfortunately, in the lives of my three girls, that precious childhood time of super play did not last very long and sipping from specially-designed drinking cups gave way to more mature ambitions.

All too soon, my little darlings began to show embarrassment when attending sleepovers with miniature cartoon characters on their pillowcases, preferring instead to dress like teen singing idols, experiment with stick-on earrings, sport fancy curls and an attitude.

That was the case when my youngest daughter came home from school one spring and mentioned that her classmates were making fun of her for embracing the latest tiny trio of cartoon super sisters.

As I entered Mother Bear Mode my eyes widened, my skin turned ashen and my lips began to shrink into a tight ball. I can assure you, nothing sweet was about to come out of my mouth.

"And what did you do?" I asked.

My daughter shrugged.

"Oh, nothing. I just went to play somewhere else."

My lower lip dropped open and a fly flew out. If the same thing happened to me I might have punched somebody.

I think that many times in our lives we human beings feel mocked and attacked by society because we are a bit, well, different.

But God said He created each and every one of his children with special gifts, for special use, in his own special time.

We may be quirky today, but God might use that special personality, that odd outlook or that strange strength to create in us the perfect person for a particular ministry tomorrow.

We must remember that it is when we are willing to be the person God created us to be at the risk of being ousted from the world, that the Master Creator can transform our uniqueness into a mirror image of Himself.

Father Creator,
 Thank You for allowing us to be rejected by man and made Holy through Christ. You are always wise and ever mindful of what we need to thrive in Your Kingdom.
 Thank you, Lord. I love you.

Michelle Lovato

Now it is your turn. How can you see God in your quirkiness?

Spend a moment and thank God for your strange and wonderful qualities.

Father Creator.

Closer Than A Brother

Proverbs 18:24 (NIV)
One who has unreliable friends soon comes to ruin, but there is a friend who sticks closer than a brother.

By Michelle Lovato

I'm trying hard to be a better friend. After all, it's been years I allowed another human being more than a comfortable distance away from my bruised heart. And, even at 54 years old, I still grieve the reason.

Years and years ago, I'd developed one seriously strong sister-like friendship with one of the mothers whose children went to school with mine. This Christian woman became close.

She was my sister.

I never thought twice

about her car rolling into my driveway or her friendly entry into my home.

    We were two of a kind. We loved being together, talked at all hours of the day and night about every intimate detail of our lives. This warm oasis of love walked with me through thick and thin.

    Several years into our friendship, however, the two of us were tested.

    We were traveling down old Route 66 in California's Mojave Desert on our way to a home school writer's camp when a teenage girl hit the car I was driving nearly head on, causing a whopping 120-mile-an-hour impact that left me

trapped under my car's dash and struggling for my life.

Thankfully, she, her son and my daughter escaped the accident relatively unscathed; my daughter being second in line for injuries because she sat behind me.

Though the accident itself did not destroy us, the aftermath of the accident put two Christian women in a place of trauma and fear.

Sadly within a year, we so intensely disagreed about the accident's follow up activities that our friendship ended.

Losing her was like grieving a death. And somewhere deep inside I resolved never to let another friend that close to me again.

It's been more than 15

years since that loss and I still grieve my old friend's love and presence by my side. I tried several times to reach out.

No one can replace that special lady.

Since those days, dozens of lovely ladies reached out for my friendship and found me unwilling to allow anyone close enough to hurt me.

And for that time of my long walk without my sister I've struggled to stay connected to anyone other than the closest members of my own family.

In Proverbs 18:24 (NIV) the Psalmist David relates that he knows there is one, presumably God, that walks closer than a brother. That's a wonderful truth I have

leaned on again and again and again.

But there is something important I have not yet defined that speaks volumes about the importance of friendship.

And though I've been closed all these years, God has opened my eyes to realize that there is "something" special to be offered by many other ladies and many other friendships.

I'm glad to say, I am finally ready to give it a try.

    Author of Friendship,
Thank you that when we are unable to
        carry on in our human way, you
        are there waiting to soothe,
        heal, and walk with us,
        closer, Lord that our
        brother.
            I love you, Lord.

Michelle Lovato

Now it is your turn. Do you have a friend you lost and never recovered? Share your journey with God.

Michelle Lovato

Remember that God walks close than a brother with you. Share your praise with your most intimate friend.

Author of Friendship.

Rest for the Weary

Psalm 23: 1-3 (NASB)
The LORD is my shepherd, I shall not be in want. He makes me lie down in green pastures, he leads me beside quiet waters, he restores my soul.

By Michelle Lovato

The clock threatened to strike midnight as I lay in bed, my head atop the cool surface of a cotton pillowcase. I sighed heavily, wondering if I could count all the errands I would have to complete tomorrow.

Today proved to be a nightmare all by itself.

If it wasn't the fight of trying to deliver or pickup a kid on time, it was the constant struggle to keep my checkbook from smoking, as checks seemed to race out of there at record speed, eating money I wasn't even sure we had.

But now as the middle of the night made itself known, I was forced to stop and consider how I would manage to do it all again in the morning.

My eyes swelled as I laid there feeling overwhelmed by the demands of my life.

A stream forged its way south and I cried out to God.

"Lord. I am weak. I am tired and I don't know what to pray"

I lay there silently tongue tied as sleep crept in and carried me away. Comfortable, I rested stone still until morning. When the sun

rose over the hills and climbed majestically into the sky. I woke.

Somehow refreshed, I was ready to take on a new day.

Nothing changed from 12 hours ago. My calendar was still packed, my commitments were still dangerously close to overload. But during the night as I lay unmoved something wonderful happened.

God, who is willing and able, gave me rest, renewed my heart and rejuvenated my soul for the new day.

It did not matter that my prayers were absent of flowery words, or that I did not quote fanciful and poignant scripture. It did not depend on the quantity of Bible study I logged or how many

people I shared with during the day.
    The healing rest was up to God. It was his decision, His work. All He wanted from me was a willing heart.

    Lord of Rest,
    Thank you for your daily desire to help me rest, to renew my spirit and rejuvenate my soul. I love you.

Now it is your turn. Describe an instance where you were overwhelmed, then rejuvenated by God.

Before you rest, thank God for all he is willing and able to do.

Lord of Rest.

Stinky Slinky!

Isaiah 1:18 (NASB)
"Come now, and let us reason together,"
Says the Lord, Though your sins are alike scarlet, they shall be as white as snow; though they are red as crimson they shall be like wool.

By Michelle Lovato

The early evening sun turned to marigold as it cast its last golden glow over the horse ranch next door.

I sat in the patio shade, swinging gently in my glider wondering if God could possibly improve on the scene laid before me. A gentle breeze picked at my hair and tickled my neck and the girls whooped happily about as they shot at the basketball hoop for cookies.

Slinky, our "Pudding" Terrier, wallowed

around in the grass as if it were itching her skin. All was well with the world at that moment.

I reached to my side to pick up a recently purchased book of photographs and began scanning its pages when "it" happened.

An odd aroma infiltrated my aura. A strangely unidentified defilement circulated my space. A stifling smell reached right up and burned itself into my nostrils.

Something was fishy. No. Something smelled fishy.

I took a gentle glance around, and then a quick darting check.

It wasn't me. It wasn't the kids. And no matter how badly I

thought so, it wasn't my husband either.

And then the answer jumped right up onto my lap wagging her tiny tan tail furiously behind her.

Not to be outdone by her back half, our little stinky Slinky began a licking frenzy that could put a hyperactive woodpecker to shame.

Unfortunately for me, however, the last thing Slinky ate appeared to have leaped out of her mouth and smeared itself around thoroughly on her entire tiny body.

That dog needed a bath.

As I sent Slinky straight to my husband for a shower I couldn't help thinking that stinky Slinky must pale in an aroma comparison to sin.

The Bible reminds us that sin carries with it a horrendous stench. So horrible in fact, that because of sin, we humans were alienated from God. And it wasn't until Jesus covered our sin by dying on the cross that we were able to enter into the presence of our God once more.

Slinky needed a physical shower of water and soap, but we humans need a shower of a different type: a spiritual one of repentance and restoration that can only be given through Jesus.

>Lord of Many Missions,
> Thank You, for allowing us a path back to you through Jesus. I love You, Lord.

Now it is your turn. Does your sin stink?
Have you received a shower of redemption?
How did that feel for you?

Praise God for recognizing our odor and washing us clean through his son.

Lord of Many Missions.

Funky Fellowship Is A Family Friend

1 Thes 1:6 (NIV)
You became imitators of us and of the Lord, for you welcomed the message in the midst of severe suffering with the joy given by the Holy Spirit.

By Michelle Lovato

Since our girls were old enough to grin and goo, it's been our family's special pleasure to host funky and wild, rip roaring, hair raising praise parties wherever we could find a piece of empty floor, blast top-40 Christian music, dance, jump, wiggle and wail our worship to God.

I remember one special evening when attending a family praise party was one of the only things I looked forward to.

It was just past

Thanksgiving and I was home flat on my back.

Both my legs were recently surgically rebuilt. Two metal rods and dozens of screws permanently replaced my bones.

Six weeks earlier a young teenage girl driving at 78 mph crossed over the median of a local street and hit my car nearly head on.

Three times the horrible reality of death loomed perilously near. But God, in his timeless wisdom, was not ready to call me home.

So after several weeks, a holiday and a lot of sleep, I sat in my wheelchair for one of the first times, grinning like a goonie bird, crying and smiling, laughing and praising the good Lord who knows all my needs.

As I watched my precious girls dance,

twist and jump around the living room my heart nearly leaped from my chest in amazement of God's goodness.

The eldest and youngest clasped hands and hurled themselves around, jumping to the loud worship tunes while my middle child pushed my wheelchair back and forth on the brown fuzzy carpet, which was her way of dancing on wheels.

Though the accident left me crippled and financially ruined, my Savior, my Jesus, left me happy to be alive.

How glad I am to have these beautiful girls to raise and how glad I am to praise my Jesus.

Dear Author of Love,
Thank You for Your glory
that I might stand near
the glow of it and be

Michelle Lovato

amazed at Your infinite wisdom and beauty.
Thank you, Lord. I love you.

Now it is your turn. What circumstance left you happy to be alive?

Michelle Lovato

Thank God, the Author of Love for penning your love story.

Author of Love,

Free To Run To Jesus

Colossians 3:23 (NASB)
Whatever you do, do your work heartily,
as working for the Lord, not men.

By Michelle Lovato

I was standing outside my home the day I noticed a friend running toward me. Though I am not usually a panicker,. she called out my name and I ran toward her thinking she must be in distress. I darted from side to side not sure if I should get my keys, my husband or my money.

"I need you," she yelled. "Come and, run this last mile with me."

In a flash I remembered Heidi was training for a marathon. It took her four long hours to run the first 17 miles of her day's training.

She was down to the last mile and she needed a friend to help her finish. Despite her desire to finish, Heidi's body was tired and she was running that distance with all her heart.

There are not too many people in the world dedicated enough to endure the relentless training it takes to complete a 26-mile marathon, the months and months of building endurance and distance for the purpose of one exhausting future day.

But, like my friend, there are those willing to pay the price that comes along with that stressful and ultimately rewarding all-encom-

passing dedication.

As children of the sovereign God Most High, we need to remember Jesus Christ paid the ultimate price for our entrance to eternity through his life and death on the cross.

Jesus is a perfect example of complete dedication.

Whether it's training for a marathon, building a prayer life, or simply stealing away a few minutes each day with God, we need to be like my marathon-running friend and work at it with all our hearts.

And if we get down to the last mile, fatigued and in need of a friend, we can be assured that Jesus Christ is willing to help all who call on him to reach the finish line.

Father Friend,

Thank you for being my ultimate ally. You understand intimately the marathon I am running because you ran it before me, and knew I would need your help.

Thank you for your sacrifice and understanding, as well as your eternal willingness to run every mile of life with me.

Now it is your turn. How can you see God in your circumstances?

Whether your life circumstances are good or bad, share your heart with God.

Lord of Riches,

Not So Big, After All

Psalm 139:13-14 (NIV)
You created my inmost being; you knit me together in my mother's womb. I praise you because I am fearfully and wonderfully made; your works are wonderful, I know that full well.

By Michelle Lovato

Some people say I am "Larger Than Life," but I know that truthfully speaking, I am just larger than my pants.

Now I must admit that having the tendency to stretch my waistband over the years has forced me to create certain, well, teeny tiny tales about my disposition while denying my growing girth that has exaggerated about as far as the elastic embedded half way between my mouth and the floor.

It's not that I want to fib or anything.

It's just that I noticed

some time ago that in order to maintain my hour-glass figure I was going to have to either stand in front of a carnival mirror or create a clothing distraction that would confuse others so much they wouldn't want to look in my cereal box to find the surprise inside.

I must admit there were times in my life when I honestly tried to loose the extra fluff, but it wasn't long before I got tired of squeezing into that sweaty Velcro waist reducer.

But God says that we are not to worry about such things. We are wonderfully made, uniquely majestic creations, poems written by the

hand of the Great Almighty, artwork perfected by the Master Creator for His good purpose. God never fibs, never even stretches the truth.

Isn't it nice to be so loved by God?

Lord of my body,
Thank You for loving the things about me that I can not stand. Thank You for creating me wonderfully and reminding me that I am Your art work.

Now it is your turn. How do you see God in your doily form? Are you wonderfully made?

Claim the promise of God's love for you by thanking him for all life's challenges

Lord of My Body.

Jail House Rock

Psalm 86:1 (NIV)
Bend down, O Lord, and hear my prayer; answer me for I need your help. Protect me, for I am devoted to you. Save me, for I serve you and trust you. You are my God.

By Michelle Lovato

Sitting in a jail house waiting room was the last activity I dreamed I'd ever do. Yet still, here I was in this dank mint-green cube that smelled like body odor and was decorated with heavily-repainted metal furniture.

How did this happen? I thought.

Why?

My family member waited in a separate room: brick painted with a thick yellow goo.

I could not believe my position in life.

Surreal.

Finally, the appointed time arrived for me to share a conversation with my family member. After I was frisked and passed through the mandatory metal detector, I was led into a dank room with a giant glass shield, three phones and a giant tub of sanitary wipes.

I picked up the phone and started reading.

"Bend down, O Lord, and hear my prayer; answer me for I need your help.

Protect me, for I am devoted to you.

Save me, for I serve you and trust you.

You are my God."

I shouted into the barely-working phone receptacle hoping that words bouncing off the poor speakers and rubber walls behind me would pierce the glass and burn into his conscience. As I read to

him I read to myself, begging God to intervene.

I finished all 17 verses of Psalm 86 and looked back into his defeated eyes.

"This is my only comfort and my fervent prayer." I said as his eyes watered.

There was nothing else to say. The world is full of corruption, especially in politics. Only God could help now.

The good news is that God did help. My family member survived the outrageous experience and withstood the test before him.

The lesson he learned changed his future and mine as well. But the infusion of God's powerful and comforting words changed us rocked our worlds. We no longer wondered if we could stand in the fire of the enemy if God was by our side.

And that is the point. God IS by our side.

Father Justice,
    Thank you that your heart is displayed so clearly in your word, the Bible. Thank you that I can open it's cover, turn its pages, read it's words and be instantly intimate with the knowledge and love of you. Thank you for your strength of character that shows in our weakest moments and the resolve to see us through the deepest pits of our lives.
    Thank you, Lord. I love you.

Now it is your turn. Share your story of jail house rock.

Praise God as you share the revelations of your heart.

Father Justice,

Twists of Fate

John 16:13 (NIV)
I have told you these things, so that in me you may have peace. In this world you will have trouble. But take heart! I have overcome the world.

By Michelle Lovato

Ever get the feeling that the minute you turn your back someone will be there with a freshly-sharpened knife ready to plunge it in?

That never-comfortable-to-relax feeling plagued me recently.

God blessed me with a new job. It was a gift that I struggled to realize was given to me.

Finally, after six weeks of successful work, I'd convinced myself to stop waiting for the "other proverbial shoe to drop" and relax. Knowing God was in control.

I'd chosen to believe I was safe from politics and administrative budget cuts. unexpected scheduling changes and a dozen other concerns. I allowed myself instead, to move merrily along through my regular work day feeling free, for the first time, in a long time, to enjoy the moment of expressing my skill in the workplace without fear of condemnation.

Boom. Just like that. In the short moment it took for my boss to open my door, life changed. And the shoe, dropped.

In the hours and days after that experience God revealed a host of comforting truths:

God knew my boss' anguish about revealing

her news. She knew it would send me into a tailspin. And it did.

God placed my impending trauma in the form of a friend's dream before hand, telling her I would soon be in great need. My friend was there for me in the aftermath.

God graciously made it impossible for me to access any kind of emotional or physical escape in the hours that followed, keeping me from saying something damaging to innocent souls trying to reach out to me.

And God reminded me that he is the perfect place to unload my emotions and fears about my unforeseen dismissal.

Life stings.
It kills.
It harasses and confuses
and wraps me in tangles.

But God calms.
God sooths.
God renews.
God prepares and provides for tomorrow. And that makes the sting of life a little more tolerable.

Jehovah Rapha.
You are my God and you love me. Thank you that you are the God that heals. Lord thank you that you know when I am spiritually sick and that others around me are plagued with illness as well. Lord thank you that you take the sting and overcome any obstacle that might be produced by it. I love you.

Now it is your turn. Describe how you feel insecure in God's love?

Thank God that he is the healer of your body, mind and soul. Thank God that he is in control.

Jehovah Rapha.

Personal Space

Isaiah 26:9 (NIV)
My soul yearns for you in the night; in the morning my spirit longs for you. When your judgments come upon the earth, the people of the world learn righteousness.

By Michelle Lovato

As a young woman I struggled with other people entering into my personal space.

And anyone with children knows that any semblance of a mother's personal space vaporizes the moment they enter childbirth labor.

Eighteen hours before I gave birth to my first child I forgot all about the antiseptic smell of the hospital room. Once I took off my clothes and allowed a half dozen random strangers to stick tubes, wires, stickers and their own hands in just about every nook and cranny of my body. I gave up on bothering with the idea of modesty.

Before my child opened her mouth and screamed for the first time, I'd been invaded so thoroughly. I did not care what body part was hanging out to shine for all the world to see.

Little did I know, back in 1987 after I'd prepaid $600 for the birth of my child that God had a different thought process.

I will never forget the fear in that moment went a nurse rushed out of the room and another rushed in with the doctor and told me my precious little girl stopped breathing.

Bing, bam, boom.

Three minutes later, I was mother to the most incredible little girl I'd ever seen.

Though I'm not too thrilled about taking my clothes off and spreading my body out for a group of strangers, I was very glad they were willing to enter my personal space and save the life of my precious child.

God is personal. He's attracted to my heart. He knows when it is bleeding and he knows when it is in dire trouble.

God is so personal that he yearns for intimacy. God yearns so hard, that instead of trying to escape my insides, he wants to fill them up and live within me.

Imagine that. How much more personal can you get?

Lord of my Insides,

I just cannot imagine your desire to live in me, but thank you for yearning for me when I had no clue I was in need.

Thank you for love me from the time you created me and compelled me to escape my mother's womb. Thank you for loving me throughout eternity.

I love you.

Now it is your turn. Describe a time when God got into your personal space and changed your life.

Thank God that in the good and bad times, he is personal.

Lord of my Insides.

Cheap Chocolate No Match For Jesus

Matthew 8:26 (NIV)
He replied, "You of little faith, why are you so afraid?" Then he got up and rebuked the winds and the waves, and it was completely calm.

By Michelle Lovato

The taste of cheap chocolate and peanut-butter filling melted onto my tongue as I savored the sweet intersection of my protein bar and my morning coffee. It was the one quick moment I stopped thinking about my day's problems since I woke up, and I wished I had a dozen more chocolate bars and perfectly-warmed cups of coffee to eat away many more moments like this one.

Another bite, another sip, a deep inhalation of air that further heightened my short-term experience.

Oh Lord, how I hope Heaven is so sweet.

Just as that thought flowed through my brain, another one pushed it away.

Problems, problems, problems.

An extended sigh rolled out of my mouth. "How will I get through this day." I thought.

As I drank in another mouthful of post-bar coffee my eyes drifted outside.

The cloud-covered morning cloaked the sky with intimidating swirls of impending rain.

Below it I watched a small neighborhood cat scamper past my living room window and two female deer grazing quietly on the grass across the street.

Just beyond my dour outlook, I saw

calm, quiet and serenity.

My lips moved slightly north.

"Isn't that how God is?" I thought.

I see problems staring me in the face and he sees a plethora of food, safety and serenity wandering around just beyond my fears.

Jesus, confronted with terrified disciples bouncing violently on an angry sea, tells his disciples:

"You of little faith, why are you so afraid?" Then he got up and rebuked the winds and the waves, and it was completely calm."

Why wouldn't Jesus feel exactly the same way about me?

"Jesus, I prayed. Please calm my sea."

Michelle Lovato

Jehovah Sabbaoth,

    Lord my protector, thank you for your many roles in my life. Lord you know I am human and sent your son to be human and walk among us. I don't understand all the ways you work but I do know that Jesus, who was man and God, does and gave mankind specific instructions. Lord calm my sea.

Now it is your turn. Do you ever feel like your problems mounted so high you struggled to cope?

Thank the good Lord for calming your sea.

Jehovah Sabbaoth.

My Perfect Mother's Day

Proverbs 18:12 (NIV)
Before a downfall the heart is haughty, but humility comes before honor.

By Michelle Lovato

One of my favorite stories took place more than 30 years ago as my mother and I were walking along the side of a busy urban roadway.

I was a young mother just shy of a year after the birth of my first child and emerging from a rather grueling post-birth diet regimen that left me clinging to the tiniest shred of hope that I may someday actually be able to wear my favorite pants.

I proudly pushed my

adorable little girl down the highway's shoulder in her navy blue stroller, and my mother, sporting her standard early-60s peddle pushers, tennis shoes and short-sleeved blouse, strode melodiously by my side.

    As the two of us chatted about nothing important an older-model sedan passed by, and out its window, the sound of a man's wolf whistle howling caught our attention.

    A feigned frown crossed my face.

    "I hate it when guys make cat calls like that," I said betraying my outward frown, and feeling rather boosted about my latest road-

side admirer.

 I must admit that I exaggerated my walk the tiniest little bit, punching my hips just a little father to their sides.

 As fast as I could underline my last word, my mother replied.

 "Who said they were whistling at you?"

 I nearly dropped to the ground laughing right there in front of God and all our fellow citizens.

 She was right.

And, she taught me a valuable lesson.

King Solomon spent his days searching for true wisdom, and left those pearls for future generations in the book of Proverbs, where he reminds us that pride goes before destruction, and that a haughty spirit before a fall.

I can assure you. After that moment, I was no longer quite so haughty. And I loved my dear, dear mother even more for showing me that I might be just a little too proud.

God of Wisdom and Joy,
 Thank you so much for using my mom to remind me the ugliness of my youthful pride. My fall was gentle and filled me with laughter and memories I will cherish forever. I love my mom, Lord and I love you too.

Michelle Lovato

Now it is your turn. Share a time when God pointed out your haughtiness in a special way.

Thank God for his love, despite our self righteousness.

Master of My Universe.

Of Mops and Mommies

2 Corinthians 9:15 (NIV)
Thanks be to God for his indescribable gift!

By Michelle Lovato

I noticed the primary colors of Mylar balloons as I cruised by my local elementary school today.

The dancing yellow, red and blue helium balloons bounced in the air to advertise "Family Fun Day," something designed and promoted by my town's local mother's preschoolers group.

Dozens of cars with car seats flooded the parking lot and a mother leading her three small toddlers into the building caught my eye.

I felt my lips curl and my weathered eyes smile as a precious and joyful memory replayed through my mind.

Wonderful Wednesday.

The morning of the Christian Mother's Network; that happy, contented three-hour morning when angels at my local church entertained my three toddlers, and I received the gift of just a little precious time away.

It's funny now, how I don't even remember those free hours; what messages we heard, what personal growth I obtained.

What I do remember, however, is an all-too-short oasis of peace from the family's urgent

needs, and existing among of group of mothers around me feeling precisely the same way.

God is a wonderful gift giver.

He knows when it is time to usher another loving adult into the chaotic world of being mommy and relieve the tension that life itself can press down at a crushing rate.

Now that my children are grown and my grandkids are toddlers and active young children, I can return to this topic with a warm-hearted smile, an understanding soul and the willingness to donate my time so my grand children's' mothers can take a few precious hours to renew themselves, just like I did more than 25 years ago.

Father my Precious Relief From Tension,
 Thank you for your heart for us and the knowledge that at the time when I was a young mother, emotionally spent and physically drained that you were there to give me the gift of rest.
 Thank you that you provided wonderful friends to cushion the pressure of life. And thank you that now I can appreciate your love and pass that gift on to others. I love you, Lord

    Now it is your turn. Describe an experience of rest from life's burdens.

Share the joy of rest in our Father through praise.

Father my Precious Relief From Tension.

Joyful in Hope

Romans 12:12 (NIV)
12 Be joyful in hope, patient in affliction, faithful in prayer.

By Michelle Lovato

The morning was stressful. Every move my husband made annoyed me.

I was stalwart in my resolve to finish a print job I volunteered to do for a friend, and regardless of how carefully I paid attention to the communication details between my computer, the networking computer and the commercial printer, I failed.

Such an easy little chore, but not today.

My 10-minute job turned into two hours of frustrating, teeth-grinding displeasure that never

fully resolved.

Worse, when I did finally get something less than what I'd planned together, I got a phone call that my print job was no longer needed.

Whether it was the green tint in the whites of my eyes or the tightly-clenched button riding at the bottom of my face, I don't know.

All I do know is that my husband was smart enough to recognize my stress and get out of my way.

"I'm two hours off! I will never get all this stuff done!" I ranted. "We were suppose to be out of here 90 miutes ago."

My husband, calmly

walked outside, started the car, the heater and the radio. Then he returned to the house, grabbed my coffee, handed me my coat and walked back to the car.

    Funny. Somehow, nothing he did annoyed me.

    In fact, I realized shortly after we got out of our neighborhood and onto the main road that it was his patient persistence and kind recognition of my stress that unclenched my teeth and relaxed my shoulders enough to get through the rest of my day.

    And, the Chinese lunch he treated me to did not hurt either.

Patient Master,

Thank You for your hand that moves in those around me when I am unable to maintain a sense of calm. Thank you that stressful things are momentary and you are eternal. Thank you that you love me enough to interject people into my life who can help me return home to a heart focused on you.

I love you.

Now it is your turn. Tell the story of a person who lowered your stress with patience and persistence.

Share your thanks with God for providing those who help lower your stress.

Patient Master.

Art for the Aged

Psalm 139:13 (NIV)
For you created my inmost being; you knit me together in my mother's womb.

By Michelle Lovato

I harbored a love for art from early childhood. There was something special, I thought, about telling a story through the use of one's hands.

But, by the time I reached the age of motherhood., the serendipity of transforming thoughts into inspiration on a canvas all but ceased to exist.

The shear amount of time it took me to cook, clean, pay bills, get groceries, and run kids all over pushed that silent connection between mind and hand to the side.

    Still, when the kids were quiet, or if I found myself at a loss for words, I took the opportunity to grab a pencil and begin sketching the closest thing to my eyes.

    Quietly I scratched out the prominent outline of my 6'3" husband; his big nose capped with a busy brown mono-brow; his standard mustache-beard combo and a head full of so much brown and red swirling, sparkling hair that those who knew him referred to him as Bigfoot.

    Moving into 30 years later, I still sit in the quiet of my own space, pencil and paper in hand, sketching the features I've

grown to adore.

    Years ago I spent hours learning his many lines, refining them into a likeness he hated and I loved inside and out.

    Things have changed over the years. He boasts the same mustache, same beard, same Roman nose.

    But as the years progressed, the love of my life has developed two separate eyebrows and a thinning landscape of fly-away comb-over hair laying low and close to his sunburned scalp.

    Though it takes less time these days to sketch his face, I still create a melody of familiar lines and features that remind me just how much I

continue to love and adore him.

I often wonder what God must think as he sketches our lives for us from beginning through maturity and to the end?

I love the Bible verse that says I knit you together in your mother's womb.

David, the author of that Psalm acknowledged God's signature on his tumultuous life and I understand David's admiration for God's work portrayed against man's struggle.

I think God is the master artist that created the beauty in every one of us.

Master Artist,
    I love you. I love the small glimpses of you that I see in my past, my present and the hope for my future. Thank you for the opportunity to love, and to document my beautiful life you created.

Now it is your turn. Describe how your masterpiece is created?

Thank God for who he created in you.

Master Artist.

Comfort Zone

John 14:26 (NIV)
But the Advocate, the Holy Spirit, whom the Father will send in my name, will teach you all things and will remind you of everything I have said to you.

By Michelle Lovato

Over the years I've noticed that preparing to step out of my shower has become a somewhat traumatic ordeal.

There is something about the constantly surging water, precisely tuned to my desires, massaging my back, neck and head with its unending barrage of tiny customized pellets, that makes me want to stay inside. I can't help but think about the cocoon of privacy surrounding me while I am standing in there, with my humanity hanging out all over, and the purity of quiet time away from, well, distractions.

But. Ah, yes.

Ultimately, of course, the painful reality that I must take my naked body and subject its most sensitive parts to the harsh landscape of the bathroom floor while I thrash around without my glasses looking for the towel becomes my nemesis.

Perhaps it is my disdain to leave my comfort zone for the three-second jaunt from shower to towel. Maybe it is the vortex of unreasonably icy air rushing to break my magical moments

of comfort and warmth.

Whatever it is, contemplating that harsh first step out of the shower is a lot like how I see myself stepping out in the world for God.

It's a doozy, but it's worth it.

With the help of the Holy Spirit of God who can replace my sense of cold fear with the warmth of his love, I know I can face any push outside of my comfort zone.

Now, It's time to convince my feet to move forward too.

Michelle Lovato

God of Warmth and Comfort,

    I love you. Thank you that you take me from perfectly satisfied and comfortable to life in a harsh world filled with coldness. Thank you that, in your omniscient wisdom, you sent your Holy Spirit to help me step into the unknown, to shield me from harm the outside might present. I love you, Lord.

Now it is your turn. Do you ever dread stepping out of your comfort zone to serve God? Share your heart.

Thank God that he knows all your needs and will supply you with himself.

God of Warmth and Comfort..

The Case of the Bully Chihuahuas

Proverbs 1:33 (NIV)
But whoever listens to me will live in safety and be at ease, without fear or harm.

By Michelle Lovato

They lined up like unleashed pint-sized gang members. The four leather-collared chihuahuas trotting toward me sported bulging eyes, dragging tongues and fake smiles. Their low-slug legs moved forward, intimidating as they cantered down the state park driveway toward us looking a lot like they wanted to eat us alive.

"Isn't that cute," I thought. "They look like devils but they're too small to be bad." Wandering happily along on a hot-pink leash in front of me, Zoe, my

brand new three-year-old rescue Yorkie be-bopped down the path, carefree and happy to be alive.

    I don't know if it was the bejeweled screaming'-pink harness Zoe wore or the homemade hairdo I'd given her the night before, but that squad of short-haired, quadro pups was not going to allow my little angel to pass.

    Wearing stupid smiles and happy dispositions, Zoe and I strode forward.

    Zoe wagged her tiny silver-cropped tail and moved in for the lick. But the boys in black were having absolutely NO sunshine and shot forward in a quest to remove her tongue instead.

    Though I tried finishing the sentence that already

launched from my brain to mouth. I warbled some sort of guttural gobbly-gook that did not make a lot of sense but sounded like,

"Be nice to the little doggies Zoe."

I don't know what possessed me after that moment. I yanked Zoe's harness backward so hard her little legs flew forward, her eyes grew every large and her mouth started frothing and barking like she was about to kill something.

By the time the bully chihuahuas made their way close to my legs, their owner was calling them back to their proverbial campyard and I was turned in reverse and moving stealthily in the other direction.

I learned a thing or two that day however, that neither Zoe nor I will likely ever forget: Don't assume the other guy is as

Michelle Lovato

good-hearted as you are; and if you get in trouble, don't panic because God is holding your bejeweled harness and he's ready to jerk you to safety if you are in danger.

Lord of Protection,
Thank you for adorning me in the your bejeweled way. Thank you for walking with me, for knowing my good heart and for looking out for my safety.
I love you, Lord.

Now it is your turn. Share a memory about when you faced your proverbial bully chihuahuas.

Thank God for your protection.

Lord of Protection.

Safety is at the Crossroads

Psalm 91: 1-3 (NIV)
1 Whoever dwells in the shelter of the Most High will rest in the shadow of the Almighty will say of the Lord, He is my refuge and my fortress, my God, in whom I trust. Surely he will save you from the fowler's snare and from the deadly pestilence.

By Michelle Lovato

I streaked down a busy four-lane highway this week past a young boy on a bike.

Looking a lot like he never crossed such a busy street before, the young boy, poised atop his shiny two-wheeler peered out of his neighborhood road and onto the bustling street.

Next to the boy, a carelessly nervous driver searched intently for an open place to jump into traffic and jet to her next desti-

nation. The driver did not sniff at the boy's presence and appeared to be desperate to move forward.

Concerned for the boy's welfare, I passed the pair and slowed down, watching through my rear-view mirror and hoping to find comfort in the boy's safe passage across the street.

Just as I turned my engine off and opened the door, the car burst into traffic and flew past me.

The boy, however, waited, gave me a puzzled look, dismounted his bike, found a big open opportunity for safety and calmly walked across

the street.

    Sometimes I feel a lot like that innocent boy, starting out in life, just past training wheels and sitting atop my brand new two-wheeler unsure if I'm ready to face the dangerous, bustling thoroughfares of life.

    Thankfully, like the child, I know that if I allow the needlessly dangerous things of life alone, they will take off and resolve themselves which will ultimately allow me to pass through busy thoroughfares unscathed.

    And I am thankful, too that, God has equipped me with open eyes to see, open heart to feel and open mind to is watching, waiting and open mind to

Michelle Lovato

realize that following God is always going to lead me to safety.

   Omnipotent God.
   Thank you for giving me training wheels. Thank you for taking them off and thank you for navigating my way through life's most busy thoroughfares.
   I love you.

Now it is your turn. When was a time when you needed to wait for safe passage through a dangerous thoroughfare?

Thank God for his timing in your life.

Omnipotent God.

Want to be in the next Finding Faith?

Let me introduce you to interactive community publishing!

What a wonderful time to be alive! It's time to celebrate life and live it the way God intended!

God gives the gift of writing to countless people whose words never see print.

The reality of the publishing industry is that large publishing houses must ensure their investment in an author's work will return the money the publishing house spent producing it, which means industry gatekeepers are forced to carefully assess every author's title with strict constraints.

This situation is different.

Boutique Books is a privately-owned specialty niche publisher. Our mission is to encourage and enable God's servants to share their gift through our publications.

We are looking for authors to help continue this ministry of encouragement through Finding Faith: Wellness through stories of hope and love.

In the future, this devotional will feature participating writers who share personal stories of how God's hand shaped their lives.

Boutique Books does not offer pay for devotions but that means you keep your copyright.

Boutique Books does not charge authors money for publication in Finding Faith.

If your work appears in Finding Faith, you are eligible to receive a deep discount on copies of the book. You can buy copies at a discount and sell them at their retail price, $14.99.

You make as much money from your work as you desire. When you order your copies of Finding Faith, I get a few dollars from the company that physically prints the book. That is how it works.

It is a win-win situation.

Here's the catch:

All decisions for inclusion and exclusion are decided by me.

And, you MUST follow the Writer's Guidelines.

Writer's Guidelines:

I am not a grammar bully, but your work needs to read well. Ultimately, this ministry is about God's love. Every author's job is to use their words to strengthen the message of God's love and erase their presence as the story's writer. Frankly, it's about God, not about your vocabulary. You MUST be in the right frame of mind, not overly sensitive to the professional editing process.

No payment is given to authors.

If your work appears in print, your byline and a two-to-four line biography will run as well.

Each devotion starts with a Bible verse and ends with a two-to-four sentence prayer.

Your work must be Biblically-sound to a non-denominational Born Again Christian.

Your devotion must be wrapped around one of your life experiences. This is not a sermon. This is a reflection on God's work in you.

250 and 300 words. Longer works are not considered.

Limit of three devotions per author.

You must submit your work in

Michelle Lovato

the body of an email only. No attachments, no snail mail. You must provide a three-to-four sentence biographical blurb.

After acceptance, you must be on time with copy and communication emails.

Unless the editor changed the wholesale concept or message of your work, you must be willing to be edited.

You must be fully responsible for your own marketing efforts.

A submission is just that. It is not a guarantee your devotion will run.

If you are interested in participating in Finding Faith's second volume you can submit your work to:

submissions.findingfaith@gmail.com

Enjoy the work of our sample devotions.
And don't forget to end in prayer!

What are you looking for?

John 15:5 (NIV)
I am the vine; you are the branches. If you remain in me and I in you, you will bear much fruit; apart from me you can do nothing.

By Rebecca Guilliard

My brother and I are great friends, but we have had a small amount of comradely competition about some areas of our lives. For example, gardens.

While my boys and I were visiting his family one afternoon, we all walked out to look at his garden. Immediately I noticed that although the weeds between each row had been plowed, there were weeds around each plant that would need to be pulled by hand.

I almost pointed the weeds out to him, but since I hadn't seen him in a month, I decided to wait a few minutes before offering my criticism.

We began our tour of the garden, and as we reached the row of sugar-snap peas, one of the children noticed the vines were loaded with pea pods just right for picking.

After wiping a couple on our shirt sleeves, we tentatively took our first bite.

Were they bitter and tough or sweet, crisp and juicy?

They were delicious! As I savored the crunchy sweetness of that delicious yet healthy sugar-snap, I suddenly felt ashamed.

Why am I so quick to notice and point

out the weeds in other's gardens instead of looking for fruit? The whole point of a garden is not to be weed-free but to produce fruit.

All too often I am so busy focusing on the weeds I see in a friend's life, that I miss the fact that their vines are loaded with good things like kindness, patience and generosity. We usually find what we are looking for.

After that moment is my brothers garden, I made a conscious effort to notice and enjoy the positive fruit in the lives of my friends and family. Instead of pointing to the weeds, let's point to the fruit, which in turn will make our friendships and our community a positive place to grow.

Now it is your turn. Do you see weeds or precious life-giving food in your life's garden? Is God prompting you to change the way you see things?

Thank God for the life growing in your garden and ask him to tend to your weeds.

Father Gardener.

Practice makes ... better

Philippians 4:9 (NIV)
Whatever you have learned or received or heard from me, or seen in me, put it into practice. And the God of peace will be with you.

By Rebecca Guilliard

As a child in a very tiny community in Alaska, I had the miraculous opportunity to receive piano lessons.

Long, dark Alaskan evenings, no household TV, and my excitement about practicing (along with a VERY patient family) made the perfect combination that resulted in my learning the piano well. This skill has brought me many happy returns from those invested hours.

Over the last 20 years, I have given dozens of children lessons, encouraged my church through praise and worship, accompanied choirs, played for nursing home residents, and enjoyed many hours of personal piano time.

Music is dear to my heart. So imagine my joy when my 8-year-old son burst into the house one day and announced that he wanted to play the piano. I immediately stopped washing dishes, dried my hands, and enthusiastically told him we could begin his first lesson right now.

He looked at me with complete disgust and said, "I didn't say I wanted to take lessons. I just said I want to play."

I laughed and thought to myself, That's how we all feel.

I have considered his statement often over the years and how it applies to other areas of my life besides the piano. At times I have been envious of another's skill or

accomplishments, without realizing the many hours that they spent when no one was watching working towards their goal.

While a great teacher, coach, or mentor can instruct you with knowledge on the proper technique, only hours of practice can develop the skill.

Practical advice from Galatians tells us, "Don't be discouraged and give up on doing what is good, for at the right time you will reap a harvest of blessing."

Consider today if there is an area of life where you want to see improvements. Do the work, put in the time; you will see positive results? If any of us are willing to spend dreary hours practicing in secret, we will be prepared at the right time for a shining performance.

Now it is your turn. Reflect on a time in your life when you assumed your children would love the same things you did. How does that expectation stifle them from being themselves?

Thank God for customized individuals he gave your to care for.

Father of all Personalities.

My Way, His Way

John 15:1 (NIV)
I am the true vine, and my Father is the gardener.

By Rebecca Guilliard

Early morning devotions have become a foundation cornerstone of my relationship with God. But it hasn't always been so. One morning when I was a teenager, I had the sweetest devotion time. I finished feeling encouraged and peaceful. Hooray, I thought. This will be a terrific day.

On the contrary, it turned out to be a frustratingly difficult day. And to make it worse, I could tell the situations I faced had been divinely engineered to cross my will.

Why would God seemingly punish me for making

an effort to seek Him? David the Psalmist may have found comfort and great reward from seeking God early in the morning, but it wasn't working for me! Until God, the faithful Gardener, gave me this practical illustration.

One summer I planted a large vegetable garden. Even though my mom had always made gardening look easy, I hadn't taken the time to learn her techniques. One warm summer day I could tell the garden needed water, but I thought I would pull the weeds first so that the vegetable wouldn't have to share the water with the weeds.

The first weed snapped off in my hand with the root still in the ground. The second weed did the same. After attempting to weed half a row with the same result on each weed, I gave

up, turned on the sprinkler, and went on to other chores.

Two hours later I came back to shut off the sprinkler. When I absentmindedly tugged at a weed and it slipped right out of the ground, I was amazed! In record time I weeded the whole garden.

As I finished the last row and turned to look back at my wet, weed-free garden, God spoke to my heart.

Just as the ground was soft after it had been watered, in the same way your heart is soft after you spend time with Me and have been watered by My word. It is only then that I can pull the weeds and get the roots.

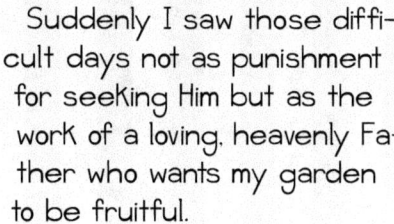

Suddenly I saw those difficult days not as punishment for seeking Him but as the work of a loving, heavenly Father who wants my garden to be fruitful.

Now it is your turn. When was the last time you decided you knew better than God? What happened?

Thank God for his great mercy and kindness toward our stubborn nature.

Father My Leader..

Author Biographies:

Michelle Lovato lives in Polson Montana with her husband of 27 years and her five lap dogs.

No. She never fathomed she would someday be "that dog lady."

Lovato has been a professional writer for 28 years and spends her days bathing tiny terriers and creating beautiful tapestries of words and thoughts. Lovato has three grown daughters, Melissa, Christian and Brandie; one son-in-law, Army Captain Shawn Cummings; and three beautiful grandchildren, Reagan, Carter and Archer.

Rebecca Gilliard lives in Bigfork, Montana with her husband Chip and two teenage sons, Logan and Bryce. She sells real estate, teaches piano lessons, and volunteers at school and in the community every opportunity possible. Her goal is to be like a movie theater popcorn machine "always overflowing with the joy and hope that comes from peace with God, that those around her can't wait to taste and see that the Lord is good."

Rebecca Gilliard lives in Bigfork, Montana with her husband Chip and two teenage sons, Logan and Bryce. She sells real estate, teaches piano lessons, and volunteers at school and in the community every opportunity possible. Her goal is to be like a movie theater popcorn machine always overflowing with the joy and hope that comes from peace with God, that those around her can't wait to "taste and see that the Lord is good."

Michelle Lovato

www.ingramcontent.com/pod-product-compliance
Lightning Source LLC
LaVergne TN
LVHW051519070426
835507LV00023B/3186